Issue #2
Fall 2008

biography for beginners

Sketches for Early Readers

Laurie Lanzen Harris,
Editor

Favorable Impressions

P.O. Box 69018
Pleasant Ridge, Michigan 48069

Laurie Lanzen Harris, *Editor and Publisher*
Dan Harris, *Vice President, Marketing*
Catherine Harris, *Copy Editor*

Favorable Impressions
P.O. Box 69018, Pleasant Ridge, Michigan 48069

Contents

Preface

Biography for Beginners is a publication designed for young readers ages 6 to 9. It covers the kinds of people young people want to know about — favorite authors, television and sports stars, and world figures.

Biography for Beginners is published two times a year. A one-year subscription includes two 100-page hardbound volumes, published in Spring (May) and Fall (October).

The Plan of the Work

Biography for Beginners is especially created for young readers in a format they can read, understand, and enjoy. Each hardcover issue contains approximately 10 profiles, arranged alphabetically. Each entry provides several illustrations, including photographs of the individual, book covers, illustrations from books, and action shots. Each entry is coded with a symbol that indicates the profession of the person profiled. Boldfaced headings lead readers to information on birth, growing up, school, choosing a career, work life, and home and family. Each entry concludes with an address so that students can write for further information. Web sites are included as available. The length and vocabulary used in each entry, as well as the type size, page size, illustrations, and layout, have been developed with early readers in mind.

Because an early reader's first introduction to biography often comes as part of a unit on a writer like Dr. Seuss, authors are a special focus of *Biography for Beginners*. The authors included in this issue were chosen for their appeal to readers in grades one through four.

There is a broad range of reading abilities in children ages 6 to 9. A book that would appeal to a beginning first-grade reader might not satisfy the needs of an advanced reader finishing the fourth grade. To accommodate the widest range of readers in the age group, *Biography for Beginners* is written at the mid-second grade to third grade reading level. If beginning readers find the content too difficult, the entry could be used as a "read aloud" text, or readers could use the boldfaced headings to focus on parts of a sketch.

Indexes

Each issue of *Biography for Beginners* includes a Name Index, a Subject Index covering occupations and ethnic and minority backgrounds, and a Birthday Index. These indexes cumulate with each issue. The indexes are intended to be used by the young readers themselves, with help from teachers and librarians, and are not as detailed or lengthy as the indexes in works for older children.

Our Advisors

Biography for Beginners was reviewed by an Advisory Board made up of school librarians, public librarians, and reading specialists. Their thoughtful comments and suggestions have been invaluable in developing this publication. Any errors, however, are mine alone. I would like to list the members of the Advisory Board and to thank them again for their efforts.

Linda Carpino   Detroit Public Library
                   Detroit, MI

Nancy Margolin McDougle Elementary School
                   Chapel Hill, NC

Deb Rothaug   Plainview Old Bethpage Schools
                   Plainview, NY

Laurie Scott   Farmington Hills Community Library
                   Farmington Hills, MI

Joyce Siler   Westridge Elementary School
                   Kansas City, MO

Your Comments Are Welcome

Our goal is to provide accurate, accessible biographical information to early readers. Let us know how you think we're doing. Please write or call me with your comments.

We want to include the people your young readers want to know about. Send me your suggestions to the address below, or to my e-mail address. You can also post suggestions at our website, www.favimp.com. If we include someone you or a young reader suggest, we will send you a free issue, with our compliments, and we'll list your name in the issue in which your suggested profile appears.

And take a look at the next page, where we've listed those libraries and individuals who will be receiving a free copy of this issue for their suggestions.

Acknowledgments

I'd like to thank Marco Di Vita for superb design, layout, and typesetting; Catherine Harris for editorial assistance; Barry Puckett for research assistance; and Kevin Hayes for production help.

Laurie Harris
Editor, *Biography for Beginners*
P.O. Box 69018
Pleasant Ridge, MI 48069
e-mail: laurieh@favimp.com
URL: http://www.favimp.com

Congratulations

Congratulations to the following individuals and libraries, who are receiving a free copy of *Biography for Beginners,* Fall 2008, for suggesting people who appear in this issue:

Sister Jeanette Adler, Pine Ridge Elementary, Birdseye, IN
Carol Blaney, Conley Elementary, Whitman, MA
Karen Locke, McKean Elementary, McKean, PA

Natalie Coughlin
1982-
American Swimmer and Olympic Champion
Winner of Six Olympic Medals in 2008,
A Record for an American Female Athlete

NATALIE COUGHLIN WAS BORN on August 23, 1982, in Concord, California. Her last name is pronounced "COG-lin." Her parents are James and Zennie Coughlin. James is a police officer, and Zennie is a paralegal. Natalie has a younger sister named Megan.

NATALIE COUGHLIN GREW UP in Vallejo, California, near San Francisco. Very early on, she showed a love and a talent for swimming.

STARTING TO SWIM: According to family legend, Natalie's parents first put her in the pool when she was just a few weeks old. She took a baby swimming class at 10 months. When she was six, she started to train and compete. She was fast, and she loved the sport. But, according to her coach, Ray Mitchell, she was a "thrasher." "The kid had one speed," he recalls. "And that was all out."

Natalie joined a swim club called the Terrapins. Soon, she was swimming year round, two practices a day. In her first big race, at the age of 13, she swam so fast she was ahead of the pace for the adult record. "This was the first indication that we had a world-class kid," says her old coach.

Soon, Natalie was working hard, building speed and endurance. She never complained or loafed. "She'd finish a hard set, and as soon as she touched the wall, she'd look up with big eyes, like, 'O.K.! What's next?'" Coach Mitchell recalls.

Natalie was great in every stroke: freestyle, backstroke, butterfly, and breaststroke. "This kid was good at everything," her coach recalled. At 15, she became the first swimmer to qualify for all 14 events in the National Championships.

But all her zeal in the pool cost her, too. "What she lacked was an internal monitor," remembers her coach. "She swam all-out when she was tired." That led to a serious injury, and almost ended her career.

A SERIOUS INJURY: In March 1999, Natalie was swimming a particularly tough practice. The coach had them swimming sets of butterfly, the most strenuous stroke there is. She swam the sets all out, trying to do her best. She woke up that night with terrible pain in her shoulder. "It was just throbbing," she recalled.

The next morning, she couldn't move her arm. She'd torn a muscle, and nearly had to quit. She spent most of the next year and a half in physical therapy. She still tried to swim, but it hurt so much. "I cried probably every single practice," she recalled.

Natalie was scheduled for surgery, but then she went to Dr. Michael Dillingham. He's a famous "orthopedist." That's a doctor who specializes in treating people with bone and muscle disorders and diseases. He helped her to overcome her injury and get back to her true form. She wasn't able to make the 2000 Olympics, but soon she was swimming faster than ever.

NATALIE COUGHLIN WENT TO SCHOOL in Concord, California. She graduated from Carondelet High School in Concord, where she was a good student and a swimming star.

COLLEGE RECORDS: Coughlin chose the University of California at Berkeley for college. That is one of the best schools in the country, with an excellent swimming program, too. She was a great student, majoring in Psychology.

Coughlin became one of the greatest female swimmers in the school's history. While in college, she won 12 NCAA titles. (The NCAA is the National Collegiate Athletic Association. That is the organization that makes the rules and regulations for college sports.) She lost only one race in her entire college career.

THE 2004 OLYMPICS: Coughlin went to the Olympics for the first time in 2004, held that year in Athens, Greece. She won five medals, one in each of her events. She won two gold medals, one in the 100-meter backstroke and one in the 4 x 200-meter freestyle relay. She won two silver medals, one in 4 x 100-meter free relay and one in the 4 x 100-meter medley relay. And she won a bronze in the 100-meter freestyle. It was an incredible accomplishment. She was only the third American woman to win five medals in one Olympics.

Coughlin kept swimming, and added some new elements to her training. She started weight-lifting, doing Pilates, and running. "I run with my dog every day," she

Coughlin poses with Dara Torres, Lacey Nymeter, and Kara Lynn Jones, the team that won the silver medal in the 4 x 100 freestyle relay, Aug. 10, 2008

says. "There's a trail right by the house, just under three miles. It's a lot of fun for both me and my dog." Her Pilates coach encouraged her to focus on things other than swimming. He told her to find "a balanced lifestyle, and a life outside the pool." It worked. "My times started to improve," she recalls. "So I just kept going in that direction, and I've been having personal bests left and right."

OLYMPIC TRIALS, 2008: In July of 2008, Coughlin made the record books again. She set a new world record in the 100-meter backstroke twice during the meet. She also qualified for the 200-meter IM. The "IM" is the "individual medley." It's one of the hardest events in swimming, and includes butterfly, backstroke, breaststroke, and freestyle.

In the 100-meter freestyle, Coughlin placed second to the amazing Dara Torres. (Torres, at 41, is the oldest woman to win an Olympic medal in swimming.) Coughlin was named U.S. Olympic Swim Team captain, a title she shared with Dara Torres and Amanda Beard.

Her performance at the Olympic trials qualified Coughlin for six Olympic events. She arrived in Beijing in August, 2008 ready to make history.

THE 2008 OLYMPICS: Coughlin went to the Olympics favored in several events. But the attention of the world was on her teammate Michael Phelps, who was favored to win eight gold medals. (You can read an update on Phelps in this issue.) Coughlin didn't mind not being the center of attention. She went out and swam her best.

Coughlin's first medal in the 2008 Olympics was a silver. She won it as a member of the 4 x 100-meter freestyle relay. Coughlin swam into the history books again on August 12th. She won the 100-meter backstroke, and became the first woman to win back-to-back gold in the event.

Coughlin won the backstroke event soon after the men's 4 x 100 relay victory. In that race, the American

Coughlin at the start of the 100-meter backstroke, Aug. 12, 2008.

men were behind the French team until the final 25 meters. Then, American swimmer Jason Lezak came from behind at a furious pace, beating out the French team. It was one of the most memorable moments in the Olympics.

Inspired by their victory, Coughlin started to cry as she received her gold medal. "I was just overwhelmed with emotion," she said. "The whole team gained a lot of emotion from the men's relay. It was probably the most amazing swim I've seen. I think it got a lot of us pumped up for the rest of the meet."

The medals just kept coming for Coughlin, as she won three bronzes, one in the 200-meter IM, one as part

15

Coughlin during the ceremony celebrating her gold medal in the 100-meter backstroke, Aug. 12, 2008.

of the 4 x 200-meter freestyle relay, and one in the 100-meter freestyle.

MAKING OLYMPIC HISTORY: Coughlin's final event of the Olympics was the 4 x 100-meter medley relay. She swam the backstroke portion of the relay, leading her team to a silver medal. It was her sixth medal of the 2008 Olympics, and gained her a place in Olympic history. She is the only American woman in any sport to win six medals in one Olympics.

The day that Coughlin won her sixth Olympic medal was the same day Michael Phelps became the first person ever to win eight gold medals. His accomplishment overshadowed hers, but Coughlin didn't mind at all. She's incredibly proud of her American teammate. "He deserves every once of respect and admiration and attention because what's he's doing is phenomenal," she said.

FUTURE PLANS: Coughlin is taking some time off now, for a well-deserved rest. She plans to keep on racing for

QUOTE

"I'm still driven to compete because I keep getting better. My times are faster, my form has improved, and I'm stronger yet more relaxed. Part of the reason is that I've learned not to take the sport too seriously. Yes, it's my profession, but life will go on if I don't win a race."

as long as she can. "Sure, after so many years, there are times I want to call it quits. But like you would do in any job, I weigh the pros and cons and then I realize I'm not ready to move on yet. I know I can still do better."

NATALIE COUGHLIN'S HOME AND FAMILY: Coughlin is engaged to Ethan Hall, who is also a swimmer. They plan to get married in the spring of 2009. She lives in Lafayette, California, with two dogs, Shera and Jake. Natalie has several hobbies. She loves to cook, and even prepared a recipe with Al Roker on the "Today" show. She says she'd like to have her own cooking show some-day. She also loves to surf and take photographs.

Coughlin is involved in charities, too. She con-tributes to the Women's Sports Foundation and is active in the Campaign for Tobacco-Free Kids.

SOME OF NATALIE COUGHLIN'S RECORDS:

Olympic Swimming

2004: Gold Medal, 100-meter backstroke, 4 x 200-meter
  freestyle relay

Silver Medal, 4 x 100-meter relay, 4 x 100-meter medley
    relay

Bronze Medal, 100-meter freestyle

2008: Gold Medal, 100-meter backstroke

Silver Medal, 4 x 100-meter freestyle relay; 4 x 100 med-
    ley relay

Bronze Medal, 200-meter IM; 4 x 200-meter freestyle relay; 100-meter freestyle

FOR MORE INFORMATION ABOUT NATALIE COUGHLIN:

Write: USA Swimming
      1 Olympic Plaza
      Colorado Springs, CO 80909

WORLD WIDE WEB SITES:

http://www.cstv.com/schools/cal/sprots/w-swim/mtt/ coughlin

http://www.usaswimming.org

Ella Fitzgerald
1917-1996
African-American Singer
"The First Lady of Song"

ELLA FITZGERALD WAS BORN on April 25, 1917, in
Newport News, Virginia. Her parents were William and
Temperance Fitzgerald. They never married, but they
lived together for several years. Her father left the family when Ella was two years old.

Ella and her mother moved to New York when she
was three. Later, her mother married a man named Joe

Da Silva. They had a daughter, Frances, who was Ella's half-sister.

ELLA FITZGERALD GREW UP in Yonkers, just north of New York City. She grew up with all kinds of kids—Irish, Italian, Greek, and African-American. She was a shy child, but she loved to sing and dance. And she knew that someday she'd be a star. "Someday you're going to see me in the headlines," she told a friend. "I'm going to be famous."

Ella started singing in the choir at church when she was in elementary school. She also started dancing with Charles Miller, the brother of her friend Annette Miller. They would make up dances and perform them for all the people of the neighborhood.

ELLA FITZGERALD WENT TO SCHOOL at the local public schools. She went to P.S. 10 in Yonkers for elementary school. Next, she attended Benjamin Franklin Junior High. She was an excellent student. She also loved to sing and dance. One friend remembered that during lunch break, Ella would stand outside the school, dancing. "She would be popping and shaking and swaying, dancing to herself," he recalled.

EARLY TRAGEDY: When Ella was just 15, her mother died. This was a dark, terrible time in her life. Her stepfather became abusive. She left home and went to live with an aunt. She dropped out of school to make money.

Fitzgerald performing in Stockholm, Sweden, Feb. 10, 1952.

Fitzgerald got in trouble, and wound up in a juvenile detention center. The New York State Training School for Girls was a terrible place. She and the other African-American girls were kept in the basement. They were treated horribly. As soon as she was released, she went to New York City. She lived on the streets and made money anyway she could.

Then, on November 21, 1934, Ella Fitzgerald got her big break.

A SPECIAL NIGHT AT THE APOLLO THEATER: On that date, Fitzgerald entered an amateur night contest at Harlem's famed Apollo Theater. She was supposed to compete as a dancer. Fitzgerald described her 15-year-old self:

"There I was, nervous as can be," she recalled. "Only 15 years old, with the skinniest legs you've ever seen. And I froze. I got cold feet. The man in charge said that I had better do something up there. So I said I wanted to sing instead."

She sang a song made popular by one of her favorite singers, Connee Boswell. It was "The Object of My Affection." The audience went wild. She won the $25 prize. More importantly, one of the greatest careers in music was launched that night.

Fitzgerald performing with Duke Ellington, Jan. 28, 1966.

A LEGENDARY CAREER: Fitzgerald's singing career lasted more than 60 years. She sang in many different styles over those years, from Big Band, to jazz, bebop, and pop. She brought her own gifts to all those types of music. She had an unfailing sense of phrasing, knowing how to bring out the meaning behind the notes and words. She could take apart the rhythm and melodic line of a piece of music, rework it, and make it her own. Her sense of pitch was unwavering, too. She could hit a note right in the middle, never off key.

Fitzgerald's career took off in 1935, when her friend and fellow musician Charles Linton introduced her to Chick Webb. Webb was the leader of a well-known Big Band.

The Big Band Era: The Big Band era of the 1930s and 1940s was named for full orchestras that played popular tunes. It's often called "swing" music, because its tunes and rhythms are great for dancing. The groups often had a major composer, like Duke Ellington, as the leader.

Fitzgerald toured the country with Webb's band. They were hugely popular. She started to make records, too. In 1938, she had her first million-seller, "A- Tisket, A-Tasket," a song she co-wrote with Al Feldman.

When Webb died in 1939, Fitzgerald became the head of the band. They toured for several years, and made records together. By then, she was performing as the featured singer with other Big Bands.

Jazz and "Scat" Singing: In the 1940s, Fitzgerald began to develop her gift for jazz singing. She learned to take apart a melody and improvise small solos. She also began to

Fitzgerald performing at Carnegie Hall, New York City, June 25, 1989.

improvise and sing nonsense syllables to tunes. That's what "scat" singing is. Scat was probably created by Louis Armstrong, but Ella was one of the best scatters ever.

Bebop: In the 1940s, jazz greats Dizzie Gillespie and Charlie Parker created a new direction in jazz with a style called "bebop." Unlike the music of the Big Bands, bebop was music to *listen* to, not to dance to. It's full of complex chords and unusual harmonies. Bebop explores the harmonic possibilities, especially in chord progressions, rather than the melodic qualities of a song.

Fitzgerald performed bebop with Gillespie, and the results were fantastic. She loved it, too. "I used to get thrilled listening to him when he did his bebop."

Norman Granz: In 1953, Fitzgerald met the record producer Norman Granz. He became her manager, and helped produce the records that made her world-famous.

Granz developed the performance and recording careers of Fitzgerald and other African-American jazz artists. He started a series of famous live concerts from the Los Angeles Philharmonic. These concerts were recorded and broadcast all over the country. They introduced a generation of listeners to some of the finest jazz musicians, including Fitzgerald. Granz also refused to abide by the segregated seating laws of the South. He made sure that all the concerts he booked allowed African-Americans the best seats in the house.

Granz helped make Fitzgerald one of the greatest recording artists ever. Over the years, she made more than 70 record albums that sold millions of copies. Under Granz's management, Fitzgerald explored some of the greatest music ever created in America.

The "Songbooks": With Granz, Fitzgerald recorded songs by some of the finest composers of the era. These recordings became her "Songbook" series. Her versions of the music of Duke Ellington, Cole Porter, Ira and George Gershwin, and others became classic collections. They were enjoyed by jazz lovers and general listeners, too.

Fitzgerald's fellow musicians admired her ability as much as her millions of fans. One of them was Ed Thigpen, who played drums for her for years. "Ella's musicianship is just incredible," he said. "Playing with her is like playing with a full orchestra. She has a vast knowledge of every song ever written, knowing all the verses, knowing what songs mean, and still interpreting them her own way. Her rhythmic sense is uncanny."

In the 1960s, Fitzgerald's audience grew as she appeared on television specials. Her fame grew around the world, as she continued to tour and record.

HEALTH PROBLEMS: In the late 1970s, Fitzgerald's health began to fail. She had diabetes. That disease can cause problems with the heart, circulation, and eyes. She began to lose her eyesight, and she had to have heart surgery. She performed for the last time in 1993. Ella Fitzgerald died after a stroke on June 15, 1996. She was mourned, and praised, by fans everywhere.

ELLA FITZGERALD'S HOME AND FAMILY: Fitzgerald was married two times. She married her first husband, Benny Kornegay, in 1941. They divorced a year later.

In 1947, Fitzgerald married the famous bass player Ray Brown. They adopted the son of Fitzgerald's sister, and renamed him Ray Brown Jr. Fitzgerald and Brown divorced in 1953, but they remained good friends and performed together for years. After her death, Brown arranged a musical tribute to her at Carnegie Hall.

Ella Fitzgerald was known worldwide as the "First Lady of Song." She is one of the finest interpreters of some of the finest songs of the 20th century. She brought the joy of her music to millions, introducing many to the rhythms of jazz and bebop. She is an American treasure, influencing generations of musicians and inspiring music lovers everywhere.

FOR MORE INFORMATION ON ELLA FITZGERALD:

WORLD WIDE WEB SITES:

http://lcweb2.loc.gov/diglib/ihas/loc/natlib.scdb.200033594/

http://www.loc.gov/loc/lcib/9708/ella.html

http://www.pbs.org/wnet/americanmasters/database/fitzgerald_e.html

Jennifer L. Holm
1968?-
American Children's Author

Matthew Holm
1974?-
American Children's Author and Illustrator
Sister and Brother Team Who Created the
Babymouse Series

JENNIFER L. HOLM WAS BORN in California around 1968. Her parents are William and Penny Holm. William was a pediatrician and Beverly was a pediatric nurse. Jennifer has four brothers, including her co-creator of the *Babymouse* books, Matthew.

JENNIFER L. HOLM GREW UP in several places. She was born in California, then the family moved to Whidby Island, near Seattle, Washington. From there, the Holm family moved to Audubon, Pennsylvania. She remembers having a dog named Ruffy and a hamster named Sneaker "who liked to curl up in my hair and fall asleep."

Growing up in a family full of boys, Jennifer loved to do the things they did. She held her own whether the activity was swimming, softball, or spitting. They all fought over the Sunday color comic section. That would be an influence on her work later.

Most of all, Jennifer loved to read. She says a neighbor remembers watching her "rake the lawn one-handed while I read a book with the other." Among her favorite authors was Lloyd Alexander.

She loved Alexander so much that she wrote him a fan letter when she was 12. She sent along her first story, "The Dragon Who Couldn't Breathe Fire." Alexander actually called her to talk to her. "I love your books!" she screamed into the phone.

JENNIFER L. HOLM WENT TO SCHOOL at Audubon Elementary, Arcola Middle School, and Methacton High School. She remembers that she had a wonderful librarian in elementary school. She says she "barely survived" middle school, but liked high school.

She did well in school and also took part in sports and other activities. She played in the marching band, competed in debate, and played lacrosse.

After high school, Jennifer went on to Dickinson College. She studied international relations, and also started taking some writing classes. Her early short stories were reviewed by her fellow classmates. They could be pretty harsh. But Jennifer learned a lot from it.

FIRST JOBS: After she graduated from college, Jennifer moved to New York City. She got a job in television and made commercials for awhile. Then, a family diary inspired a new career in children's literature.

STARTING TO WRITE FOR KIDS: A family member sent Jennifer a copy of a diary kept by her great aunt, Alice Amelia Holm. She had grown up in the little town of Naselle, Washington, near the Pacific Ocean. Reading that diary provided the "spark" for Jennifer's first book.

OUR ONLY MAY AMELIA: *Our Only May Amelia* takes place in 1899, in the Naselle River Valley. May Amelia

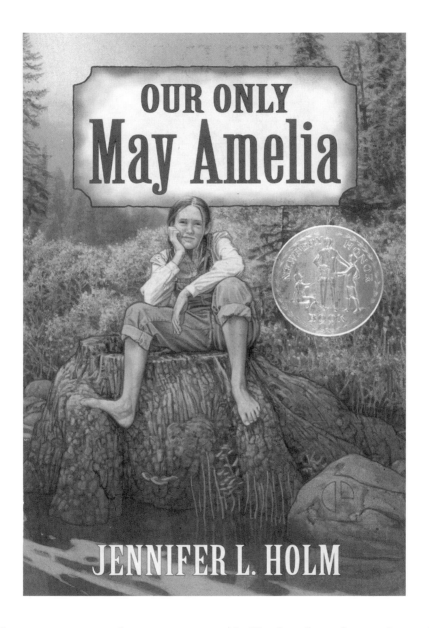

Jackson is a spunky pioneer girl. She's also the only girl in the little town of Nasel, and has to put up with seven brothers. May desperately wants a sister, but she keeps that secret to herself. Holm tells her story with humor, vividly describing May's life. Readers loved the book, and much to her surprise, Holm won a Newbery Honor. She was deeply grateful for the award. And, after her first book's success, she was able to become a full-time writer.

BOSTON JANE: Jennifer next created a series of books with another character from the past, Boston Jane. These books focus on the life of Jane Peck. Jane is 16, and has moved from Philadelphia to the wilderness of Washington state. She's feisty and fearless in her new life and surroundings.

PENNY FROM HEAVEN: Another favorite with Holm's young readers is *Penny from Heaven*. It takes place in 1953, and features 11-year-old Penny. She's trying to deal with her father's death and understand her place in the world. Her father's large Italian family helps her to discover who she is, and to appreciate her heritage. Holm based the character of Penny on her Mom, Penny Scaccia Holm. The book won Jennifer her second Newbery Honor.

MIDDLE SCHOOL IS WORSE THAN MEATLOAF — A YEAR TOLD THROUGH STUFF: One of Jennifer's recent books is about the sorrows of middle school. The main character is a 7th grader named Ginny. Instead of a simple story line, Holm presents Ginny's life in a series of doodles, post-it notes, lists, and other written pieces. Together, they form a funny, warm look at Ginny's world.

Jennifer Holm is a well-known author of her own books. But she's best known as the co-creator of the

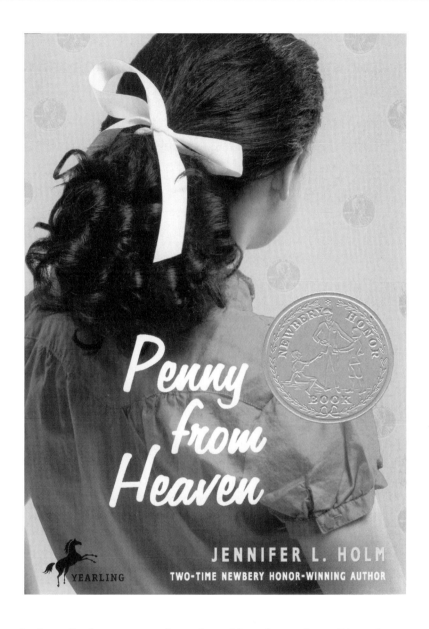

smash hit *Babymouse* books. Her brother **Matthew** is her partner in these wonderful graphic books for young readers.

MATTHEW HOLM WAS BORN around 1974 in Audubon, Pennsylvania.

MATTHEW HOLM GREW UP in a house full of lively kids. He loved sports and playing with his three brothers and one sister, and also loved comics. (They fought over the Sunday funnies every week.) He says he's known since middle school that he wanted to write for kids. "I wanted to either do a comic strip, comic books, or write and illustrate children's books."

"I consumed comic strips and comic books in prodigious amounts," he recalls. His family had collections of Bloom County, Calvin and Hobbes, Far Side, and Peanuts comics. He absorbed every one. He says he'd love to have Hobbes, from Calvin and Hobbes, as a friend. "Who wouldn't want a stuffed tiger as a best friend?" he says.

MATTHEW HOLM WENT TO SCHOOL at Audubon Elementary, Arcola Middle School, and Methacton High School. In middle school, he started drawing his own comic strips. In high school, he had a great English teacher who taught him about science fiction. He also had a terrific art teacher who guided him in his senior thesis: an illustrated children's book. It was called "The Legend of Toadspittle Hill."

Matt had another great opportunity in high school. He worked with Tony Auth, the political cartoonist of the *Philadelphia Enquirer*. He got to learn just what it takes to be a professional artist, and he loved it.

Matt went on to college at Pennsylvania State University. There, he drew cartoons for the school paper, the *Daily Collegian*.

FIRST JOBS: After college, he and a friend drove out west. On the road, they visited UFO sites all over the country. They decided to start one of the earliest online magazines. He recalls, "we decided we'd get on this wacky new thing called the World Wide Web." They called their magazine *Strange Voices*. He says it was written for "space aliens who were living on earth."

They collected their writings and published them as a book, *Gray Highways: An American UFO Journey.* For the next several years, Matt wrote articles for *Country Living* magazine. He also had a graphic art business. The experience taught him a lot about art, and about publishing, too. He says it made him ready when his sister, Jennifer, got in touch. She wanted to talk about " a comic book for girls she was thinking about, with a character called Babymouse."

STARTING THE *BABYMOUSE* SERIES: "She handed me a napkin with a scribble of a mouse on it," Matt recalls. "It had all the essential elements of Babymouse—the dress with the heart on it, hands on hips, slightly irritated expression. I took the sketch home and drew a proper Babymouse in a couple of poses. That was the inspiration for doing a graphic novel for girls about a mouse."

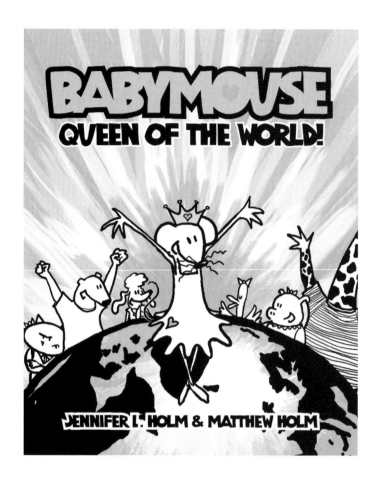

But the path to a published book wasn't easy. Jennifer and Matt first had the idea in 2001. They worked up a 50-page storyboard and took it to publishers. But no one was interested. Finally, in 2004, someone at Random House got interested. According to Matt, "the rest is history."

BABYMOUSE: QUEEN OF THE WORLD: Babymouse burst upon the world in 2005. The loveable little mouse with the vivid imagination, who loves pink, cupcakes, and books became a favorite everywhere. Young read-

ers delight in her daydreams of "Fame! Fortune! Tasty snacks!" They know how tough it is to deal with meanies like Felicia Furrypaws, while still wanting to get invited to parties. And they love the way Babymouse sticks to her true friends, like Wilson, while learning she is truly Queen of the World.

BABYMOUSE: OUR HERO: Babymouse returned again in *Our Hero*. Once again, she's late for school, and has to deal with fractions, Felicia, and Dodgeball. She faces

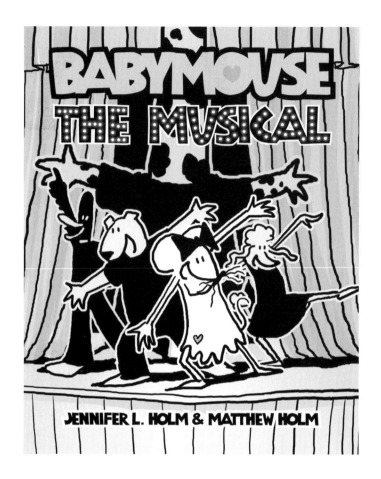

Felicia again, and isn't afraid to become a hero, even when she forgets her sneakers.

CAMP BABYMOUSE: The Mouse Queen has appeared in 10 books so far. Another favorite with her many fans is *Camp Babymouse*. In this adventure, Babymouse tries her best to be good at all the activities at camp. Of course, all sorts of things go wrong. But in the end, Babymouse makes friends, has fun, and even wins a contest.

The two most recent books featuring the delightful Babymouse show her celebrating Halloween and appearing in the school musical. Her many fans look forward to each new book.

FUTURE PLANS: Jennifer and Matt plan to write *Babymouse* books for years to come. They also have their own projects. Jennifer is continuing to write novels, and Matt has a graphic design business. He says he's really busy at the moment, working with his sister on a Babymouse-like series for boys, called *Squish, The Amazing Amoeba!*

JENNIFER L. HOLM'S HOME AND FAMILY: Jennifer lives in Maryland with her husband, Jonathan Hamel,

QUOTE: JENNIFER

"I grew up imagining that authors lead glamorous lives full of excitement and adventure. You know, traveling to exotic places, and meeting all sorts of famous people! Now that I am a writer, I know the real scoop."

QUOTE: MATTHEW

"We're asked all the time if we have problems working together, but it's never been a problem at all. We take criticism well and are able to recognize when someone has come up with an idea that makes the project better. We work long-distance almost exclusively, sending drafts and drawings back and forth. (Actually, it's kind of nice to be able to hand things off to the other person and not have to think about the work for a week or a couple of hours or whatever—it keeps you from going crazy and getting tunnel vision.)

"And as for us being brother and sister, well, that's never been a problem, either.

"Or maybe it's just because I'm so sweet that she can't help but get along with me."

and their son, Will. Jennifer and Jonathan have written a book about a cat who is a detective, called *The Stink Files.* She says they also have a "big fat black cat named Princess Leia Organa." In her spare time, Jennifer still loves to read. She also enjoys jogging, video games, and watching movies.

MATTHEW HOLM'S HOME AND FAMILY: Matt lives with his wife in Portland, Oregon, with a dog and a ferret.

SOME OF JENNIFER HOLM'S BOOKS:

Our Only May Amelia
Boston Jane: An Adventure
Boston Jane: Wilderness Days
Boston Jane: The Claim
The Creek
Penny from Heaven

***BABYMOUSE* BOOKS (BY JENNIFER AND MATTHEW HOLM):**

Babymouse: Queen of the World #1
Babymouse: Our Hero #2
Babymouse: Beach Babe #3
Babymouse: Rock Star #4
Babymouse: Heartbreaker #5
Camp Babymouse #6
Babymouse: Skater Girl #7
Babymouse: Puppy Love #8

Babymouse: Monster Mash #9
Babymouse: The Musical #10

FOR MORE INFORMATION ABOUT JENNIFER HOLM:

Write: Random House Children's Books
1745 Broadway, 10th Floor
New York, NY 10019

WORLD WIDE WEB SITES:

http://www.booksense.com/people/archive/holm
jennifer.jsp

http://childrenslit.com/childrenslit/mai_holm_jennifer.
html

http://www.jenniferholm.com/

FOR MORE INFORMATION ABOUT MATTHEW HOLM:

Write: Random House Children's Books
1745 Broadway, 10th Floor
New York, NY 10019

WORLD WIDE WEB SITES:

http://www.babymouse.com

http://www.powells.com/kidsqa/holm.html

http://www.randomhouse.com/kids/catalog/author

Langston Hughes
1902-1967
African-American Poet, Short Story Writer, and Playwright
Leading Figure of the Harlem Renaissance

LANGSTON HUGHES WAS BORN on February 1, 1902, in Joplin, Missouri. His parents were James and Carrie Hughes. They were both bookkeepers. His parents separated when he was very young.

LANGSTON HUGHES GREW UP in several different places. James Hughes moved to Mexico when Langston was an infant. He and his mother went to visit James and arrived just as an earthquake rocked the city. Langston and his mother returned to Kansas. After that, his parents divorced.

Langston's mother needed to find work. She sent him to live with his grandmother in Lawrence, Kansas, while she looked for a job.

LEARNING HIS AFRICAN-AMERICAN LEGACY: Those years living with his grandmother were important ones for Langston. He learned about his rich family heritage. He had black and white ancestors. Some had been slaves, and some had been slave owners. He learned the legacies of slavery and the Civil War.

Langston's beloved grandmother was the first black woman to attend Oberlin College. His grandfather had been part of the Abolitionist movement, the crusade to abolish slavery. He had joined fiery abolitionist John Brown in the raid on Harper's Ferry and had died there.

Langston's grandmother opened his eyes and his heart to African-American history. He learned about the brutality of slavery. He learned about the lives and hopes of working people. His grandmother took him to hear educator Booker T. Washington. Years later, Hughes would write a poem about Washington and his path from slavery to achievement.

In addition to the stories from his family's past, Langston's life was steeped in the music of the African-American community. The spirituals of the black church, and the blues music of the black community were woven into his daily life. Later, when he became a poet, they would surface again, as themes and rhythms in his verse.

Pen and ink drawing of Hughes by Winold Reiss, 1927.

LANGSTON HUGHES WENT TO SCHOOL at the local public schools in Kansas. At school he was seated at the back of the classroom, with the other black students.

When Langston was 12, his grandmother died. His mother, who had remarried, sent for him. So Langston moved to Lincoln, Illinois, to live with his mother and her new husband, Homer Clark.

In Lincoln, Hughes finished elementary school. His fellow students elected him "class poet." The family moved to Cleveland, Ohio. There, Hughes attended Central High School. He did well in school, and was editor of the yearbook.

"THE NEGRO SPEAKS OF RIVERS": Hughes wanted to attend college, but his mother couldn't afford it. He went to visit his father in Mexico. On the train, he wrote one of his first poems. As he crossed the Mississippi River, the 19-year-old poet thought about the meaning of rivers and black history.

The poem, "The Negro Speaks of Rivers," talks about ancient rivers, like the Nile in Egypt, where black people have lived, and suffered in slavery. It describes the Mississippi, where Abraham Lincoln became convinced that slavery must end. "My soul has grown deep like the rivers," is the last line of this powerful poem. It was published in the NAACP's magazine, *Crisis*, in 1921. Hughes dedicated the poem to the prominent writer and scholar W.E.B. Du Bois.

Hughes lived with his father in Mexico for a year. He briefly taught English to the children of wealthy Mexicans. Returning to the U.S., Hughes started college at Columbia University in 1921. His father wanted him to study engineering. But Hughes didn't like his classes. He left Columbia after one year. He wanted to see the world.

TRAVELING THE WORLD: In 1923, Hughes joined the crew of a boat bound for Africa. He worked as a ship's

cook. Once they arrived, he traveled through Africa and Europe, working as a dishwasher to pay his expenses. He wrote stories and poems and sent them home to be published. He returned to the U.S. in 1924.

Hughes published his first poetry collection, *The Weary Blues*, in 1926. The title poem describes a weary black piano player. With "his ebony hands on each ivory key," the man plays the "Sweet Blues, Coming from a black man's soul."

Hughes returned to college in 1926. He spent the next three years at Lincoln University in Pennsylvania. That was one of the first all-black colleges in the U.S. While taking classes, Hughes continued to write and publish poems and prose. An important influence on this early work was the poetry of Paul Laurence Dunbar. He also spent all the time he could in New York, absorbing the atmosphere of Harlem. He published his first novel, *Not Without Laughter*, in 1929.

When he graduated from Lincoln, Hughes wanted to get a job in publishing and use his writing talents. By that time, he was a published poet and novelist. But doors open to white people were closed to him. Hughes decided to move back to New York and make a living as a writer on his own terms.

THE HARLEM RENAISSANCE: Hughes was part of a group of African-American artists who formed the Harlem Renaissance. The group was based in the Harlem section of New York City. In their poetry, prose, plays, and art work, they celebrated the African-American experience. They used different styles and methods in their works, but shared a common goal. They wanted

Poetry for Young People

Langston Hughes

Edited by
David Roessel &
Arnold Rampersad

Illustrated by
Benny Andrews

to create art by black Americans that showcased their talents and dreams.

TRAVELING AND SPEAKING: Hughes visited the noted educator Mary McLeod Bethune at her college in Florida. She encouraged him to tour the South and hold poetry readings. He did, and audiences loved his work.

Hughes next traveled to the Soviet Union with several other African-Americans. He found much to praise in the country, which seemed to him free of the racism in America.

WRITING PLAYS, POEMS, AND STORIES: Back in the U.S., Hughes continued to write poems, as well as short stories and plays. His subjects were the people, places, and ways of life that he knew. He founded a theater group, the Harlem Suitcase Theater. His plays ran on the weekends, and admission was just 35 cents. They were written for working black people, who loved them. He founded similar theaters in Los Angeles and Chicago.

Yet some members of the black community didn't like Hughes's work. He tried hard to duplicate the language of simple folk. Some people objected to that. They thought he should feature educated blacks who'd achieved success. But that wasn't for Hughes. "I felt that the masses of our people had as much in their lives to put into books as did those more fortunate ones," he said. He wanted to show the lives of "the people I had grown up with."

Hughes championed other African-American artists, too. William Grant Still was an African-American composer. He was the first black to have a symphony he wrote performed by a major orchestra. Hughes wrote the words for an opera that Still composed, *Troubled Island*. It opened in New York in 1949. In the 1950s, he wrote poems to be read to jazz music. He recorded some of these with music contributed by jazz musician Charles Mingus.

JESSE B. SIMPLE: Hughes wrote a series of columns for the *Chicago Defender* about a character named "Jesse B. Simple." Simple became one of Hughes's most famous creations. He is a storyteller who lives in Harlem. He tells his stories of African-American life to a writer named Boyd. Simple is funny, warm, and open. He became the main character in a book of Hughes's short stories, *Simple Speaks His Mind.* Simple reappeared in two more short story collections and a play.

BOOKS FOR YOUNG READERS: Hughes also wrote books for young readers. Most of them were histories and biographies of famous African-Americans. He wrote collections of poems for young readers, too. *The Dream Keeper and Other Poems* is one of these collections. His poems are still read, studied, and enjoyed today by young people all over the world.

"HARLEM: WHAT HAPPENS TO A DREAM DEFERRED?" One of Hughes's most famous poems is called "Harlem," published in 1942. It is also known by its famous first line: "What happens to a dream deferred?" In the poem, Hughes talks about the dreams and hopes of African-Americans. When a dream is "deferred" (made to wait) what happens then?

> What happens to a dream deferred?
> Does it dry up
> Like a raisin in the sun?

The last lines are dark and threatening:

> Maybe it just sags
> Like a heavy load.
> *Or does it explode?*

The poem shares the themes and simple language of much of Hughes's poetry. Its powerful message tells of the seething frustration of people denied their right to hope for a better future. Lorraine Hansberry used a line from this famous poem as the title of her famous play, *A Raisin in the Sun.*

In the 1950s, anti-Communist fervor gripped the country. Blacks like Paul Robeson and W.E.B. Du Bois were condemned for their pro-Communist leanings. Because he had spoken positively of the Communist Soviet Union in the 1930s, Hughes also was condemned. He defended himself by saying he no longer held the same opinions of the Soviet Union. Some activists found his new stance unbelievable. They thought he was saying whatever he had to, to protect himself. In the eyes of some African-Americans, his reputation fell.

Hughes continued to write poems, stories, essays, and plays until his death in 1967. As he grew older, the fight for Civil Rights grew more militant. In the 1960s, some African-American activists accused him of being uncommited to the cause. Yet he remained steadfast in his strong pride as an African-American. He refused to let rage at racism overcome him. Instead, he continued to celebrate African-American life as he knew it. He felt he could condemn injustice in poetry that could remain positive about the hope for equality for all.

LANGSTON HUGHES'S HOME AND FAMILY: Hughes spent most of his adult life living in Harlem, on East 127th Street. He never married or had children. He died of cancer on May 22, 1967, in New York. His home is now a landmark, and East 127th Street is now Langston Hughes Place.

Langston Hughes is considered one of the finest poets of the 20th century. His poetry contributed to the flowering of the Harlem Renaissance. His simple, musical verse contained deep, important themes. His poetry celebrated African-American life and condemned the racism and injustice that would limit that life. His deeply affecting poetry featured the lives of the "low-down folks" he knew so well. He celebrated them in verses full of the rhythm of blues and jazz, in poetry that continues to inspire new generations.

FOR MORE INFORMATION ON LANGSTON HUGHES:

WORLD WIDE WEB SITES:

http://www.americaslibrary.gov.cgi-bin/page.cgi/aa/
  writers/hughes

http://www.poets.org/poet.php/prmPID/83

John McCain
1936-
American Politician and
Republican Candidate for President

JOHN MCCAIN WAS BORN on August 29, 1936, in the Panama Canal Zone. His full name is John McCain III. His father, John McCain Jr., was a Navy officer, who was serving in Panama when John was born. His mother, Roberta, was a homemaker. John has an older sister, Sandy, and younger brother, Joseph.

JOHN MCCAIN GREW UP grew up on Navy bases all over the world. He admits he had quite a temper growing up. When he was two, he threw violent tantrums. Sometimes he'd hold his breath, and pass out. His worried parents decided to put him in a tub of cold water at the first sign of trouble. That did the trick.

McCain grew up in a family with military heroes dating back hundreds of years. One ancestor served under George Washington during the Revolutionary War. His father and grandfather were admirals in the Navy. Their honor, patriotism, and sacrifice shaped his life.

"My family's history was my pride," he recalled. "When I heard my father or one of my uncles refer to an honored ancestor or a notable event from our family's past, my boy's imagination would conjure up some future glory when I would add my own paragraph to the family's legend."

JOHN MCCAIN WENT TO SCHOOL on naval bases all over the world. Sometimes, it was hard. He'd move to a new base, make friends, start school, then have to move again. He got to be a rebellious kid, often getting into fights. "At each new school I became a more unrepentant pain in the neck," he recalls.

John's parents sent him to an exclusive private high school. At Episcopal High in Alexandria, Virginia, he rebelled against authority again. He broke the dress code and curfew rules. He did well in his English and history classes. He didn't do well in math or science. He also played sports, including football and wrestling.

When it came time for college, McCain followed in his father's and grandfather's footsteps. He attended the Naval Academy at Annapolis. Once again, he was a rebel instead of a student. He got into trouble often, breaking rules and partying. He recalls "marching many miles for poor grades, tardiness, messy quarters, slovenly appearance, and sarcasm." McCain graduated from the Academy in 1958 and became a naval officer.

A NAVAL OFFICER: McCain moved to Florida and began his training as a Navy pilot. At first, he kept to his old ways. "I loved flying," he recalls. "But not much more than I loved to have a good time." Gradually, though, he changed his attitude. He wanted to lead men, and to gain honor in battle. "Nearly all the men in my family had made their reputations at war," he recalled.

THE VIETNAM WAR: At that time, the U.S. was getting involved in Vietnam. In the late 1950s, Vietnam was fighting a civil war. This was during the "Cold War." After World War II (1939-1945), the Soviet Union and the U.S. became the two strongest nations in the world. They represented two very different political systems. The U.S. was a democracy; the Soviet Union was a Com-

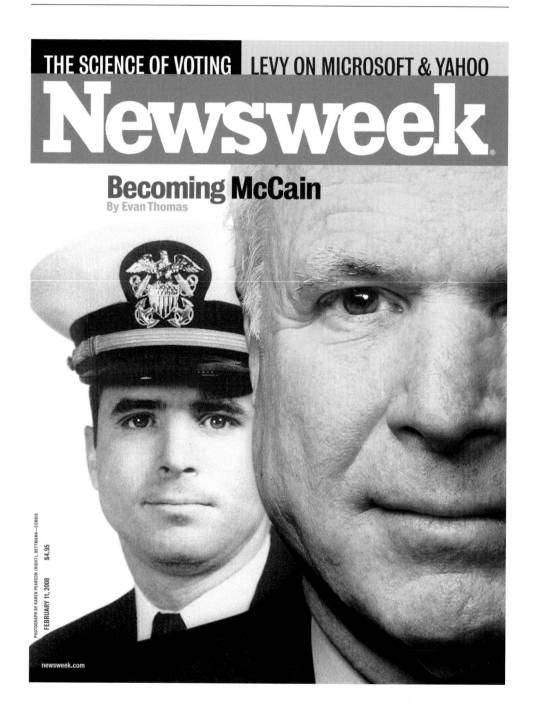

THE SCIENCE OF VOTING LEVY ON MICROSOFT & YAHOO

Newsweek

Becoming McCain
By Evan Thomas

PHOTOGRAPH BY KAREN PEARSON (RIGHT), BETTMANN—CORBIS FEBRUARY 11, 2008 $4.95

newsweek.com

McCain on the cover of Newsweek, *Feb. 11, 2008.*

munist state. For more than 40 years, the hostilities between these two nations affected world politics.

In Vietnam, the North was supported by the Soviet Union. The South was supported by the U.S. By the mid-1960s, there were hundreds of thousands of U.S. troops fighting in Vietnam on behalf of the South. Thousands of tons of bombs were being dropped on targets in the North.

FIGHTER PILOT: McCain went to Vietnam in 1967, as a bomber pilot. He flew bombing missions over North Vietnam. On his 23rd mission, on October 26, 1967, McCain's plane was shot down over Hanoi, the capitol of North Vietnam. He ejected from the plane, and broke both arms and one leg as he landed.

He was soon surrounded by a group of North Vietnamese who beat him. One broke his shoulder. Another bayoneted him in the groin and ankle. A truck appeared to take him to the Hoa Lo prison, called the "Hanoi Hilton" by the American prisoners held there. It would be his home for the next five years.

PRISONER OF WAR: McCain endured five years of torture and mistreatment as a prisoner of war. The prison officials refused to treat his injuries unless he gave information about his mission. McCain refused. He was beaten, starved, and interrogated over and over. He was tortured and his broken arms were never treated.

Because of his injuries, he cannot lift his arms above his head now, and walks with a limp.

At several points, his captors thought he would die. In fact, his family was told he was dead. McCain was put in solitary confinement. For two-and-a-half years, he was kept alone, allowed no contact with his fellow prisoners of war (POWs). Finally, he was reunited with the other American prisoners. They kept up their spirits by memorizing the names of all the other prisoners. They would tell each other the plots of novels and movies.

Finally, in early 1973, the U.S. signed an agreement with Vietnam that ended the war. John McCain was finally going home.

COMING HOME A WAR HERO: McCain returned to the United States a war hero. He was eager to get back to work for the Navy. He spent months in physical therapy and regained his strength. Soon he was teaching Navy pilots.

In 1977, McCain moved to Washington DC. He'd been named the Liaison Officer between the Navy and the Senate. In that position, he outlined the Navy's positions and needs to the government. He liked the work and began to think about a political career.

ENTERING POLITICS: In 1981, McCain retired from the Navy. He moved to Arizona, and decided to run for

McCain speaking on immigration reform, Sept. 24, 2007.

office as a Republican. His first campaign was for a seat in the U.S. House of Representatives, in 1982. He won, and has spent the last 26 years in Washington.

SENATOR: In 1986, McCain ran for, and won, the office of U.S. senator from Arizona. He's been a senator for 22 years. Over the years, he's gained the reputation of a "maverick." He is a conservative Republican, but he has always been known as someone who works well with Democrats, too.

McCain built a reputation as someone who tried to stop wasteful spending and reform the way political campaigns are financed. He wanted to stop the unlimited flow of money into politics that benefits private interests. He and Democratic Senator Russ Feingold drafted a bill, the McCain-Feingold reform bill, in 1995. It took them 7 years, but it was finally passed in 2002.

McCain has served for years on several important committees in the Senate. These include the Armed Services Committee and the Committee on Commerce, Science, and Transportation.

RUNNING FOR PRESIDENT, 2000: In 2000, McCain decided to run for President. In American politics, Presidential candidates are selected for the Republican and Democratic tickets through "primaries." The primaries take place in many states, from January to June of an election year. In primaries, voters cast ballots for delegates who are pledged to vote for one candidate. The delegates cast their official votes at the Party's convention, held the summer before the election.

McCain introduces his running mate, Governor Sarah Palin, August 29, 2008, in Dayton, Ohio.

McCain ran as a reform candidate, and had a lot of early support. George W. Bush was the favorite, and had raised a lot of money early on. But McCain stunned Bush by winning the New Hampshire, Michigan, and Arizona primaries. Bush eventually won the nomination, and served for two terms.

RUNNING FOR PRESIDENT, 2008: In 2008, McCain decided to run again for the nomination. This time, he won the total number of delegates needed early on in the primary season. His Democratic opponent in the election is Barack Obama (you can read a profile of Obama in this issue of *Biography for Beginners*).

In August, McCain chose Alaska Governor Sarah Palin as his Vice Presidential running mate. The two candidates are traveling all over the country getting their political message out. It is: "Country First: Reform, Prosperity, Peace."

McCain is campaigning on several key issues. He has been a strong supporter of the Iraq War and believes in a strong national defense. He wants to improve the economy with a pro-growth strategy. He wants the nation to become less dependent on foreign energy and develop newer, cleaner resources.

McCain believes deeply in public service. He encourages Americans of all ages to find ways to help others in need. In September, Hurricane Gustav hit the Gulf Coast at the beginning of the Republican Convention. McCain pared back Convention events. He wanted to focus on the need of people in the Gulf region. He said, "No matter what we are, Republicans or Democrats, America needs us to do what all Americans have always done in times of disaster and challenge."

JOHN MCCAIN'S HOME AND FAMILY: McCain has been married twice. He married his first wife, Carol, in 1965. Carol had two sons, Doug and Andy, from her first marriage. McCain adopted them, and he and Carol also had a daughter, Sydney. They divorced in 1980.

In 1980, McCain married Cindy Hensley. They have four children: Meghan, Jack, Jimmy, and Bridget. Bridget was an orphan who was born in Bangladesh. The McCains adopted her as an infant. Two of McCain's sons have served in the military. He is very proud of them, but doesn't want a lot of media attention centered on them. He honors their service, and asks the media to honor their privacy.

McCain has this message for students on his web site:

QUOTE

"I believe that education will strengthen your growth and confidence. Remember, it is people like you who make the future of this nation brighter and stronger."

FOR MORE INFORMATION:

Write: Senator John McCain
241 Russell Senate Office Building
Washington, DC 20510

WORLD WIDE WEB SITES:

http://mccain.senate.gov/
http://johnmccain.com

Barack Obama

1961-
African-American Politician and Activist
First Black Presidential Candidate
Chosen by a Major Party

BARACK OBAMA WAS BORN on August 4, 1961, in Honolulu, Hawaii. His full name is Barack Hussein Obama Jr. He is biracial. His father, Barack Obama Sr., was black, from the African nation of Kenya. His mother, Ann Dunham, was white, and born in Kansas. They met when Barack Sr. won a scholarship to the University of Hawaii to study.

Obama has several siblings. He has a half-sister named Maya, from his mother's second marriage. His father also remarried, and Obama has another half-sister, Auma, and half-brothers named Roy, Bernard, George, Abo, and Mark. Another half-brother, David, died in a motorcycle accident.

BARACK OBAMA GREW UP in Hawaii. His father left the family when he was two, and his parents divorced. Barack and his mother lived with his mother's parents. Barack was very close to his grandparents, who had moved to Hawaii after World War II.

When he was six, Barack and his mother moved to Indonesia. His mother had married an Indonesian man named Lolo. The family lived near the main city of Jakarta. It was a very exotic place, and Barack remembered monkeys, a cockatoo, and even baby alligators living in the garden.

BARACK OBAMA WENT TO SCHOOL first in Indonesia. He recalls that he spent two years in a Muslim school, and two years in a Catholic school. But his mother wasn't sure he was getting the education he needed in Indonesia. She wanted him to go back to Hawaii for school. He applied and got into a private school in Honolulu.

So at the age of 10, Barack moved back to Hawaii. He lived with his grandparents, and attended the Punahou

School, a prestigious prep school in Honolulu. That same year, his father came to visit. It would be the last time they would see each other, although they did write letters over the years.

Barack did very well in school, and was a basketball star, too. He graduated from high school in 1978 and went on to Occidental College in Los Angeles. After two years at Occidental, he transferred to Columbia University in New York. He graduated from Columbia in 1983. He worked briefly for a large company, but he knew he wanted more.

By this time, he was getting interested in community organizing. He knew that there were major problems in America, especially in the big cities, and especially among African-Americans. He wanted to make a difference, to get involved and help improve their lives.

GETTING INVOLVED IN COMMUNITY ORGANIZING: In 1985, Obama got a job in Chicago with an organization called the Calumet Community Religious Conference. Over the next three years, he threw himself into organizing the community to fight the problems that poverty and discrimination had brought to the city's South Side.

He got to know the people of the community, and what their problems were. Together, they tried to improve housing, education, employment, and fight

Obama on the campaign trail.

crime. He learned a tremendous amount about the problems of urban America. He got to see firsthand the problems of African-Americans who lived without hope for a better future for themselves and their families. He also learned a lot about himself.

In 1988, Obama decided he needed more education. He wanted to go to law school, to learn more about how law and politics can help change lives. But first, he began a more personal journey. He went to Africa, to learn about his African heritage.

In Africa, he met several of his half-siblings, from his father's remarriage. He also met his grandmother, and aunts and uncles.

LAW SCHOOL: Obama began law school at Harvard in 1988. He was a great student, and he became president of the Harvard Law Review. The Law Review is a very important and prestigious publication. It is written by lawyers, professors, and students, and edited by the law students themselves. Obama was the first African-American ever to be chosen for the position.

PRACTICING AND TEACHING LAW: After graduating from law school, Obama moved back to Chicago. He started working as a civil rights attorney. He also started teaching law classes at the University of Chicago. Obama taught constitutional law. That is the study of how the federal court system, including the Supreme Court, has interpreted the U.S. Constitution.

BECOMING AN AUTHOR: Obama also published his first book in 1995. It's called *Dreams of My Father*. It is a very personal look at his life, and his journey to manhood. He explores what he learned from both his mother and father, and what his heritage means to him. He also writes about how he came to understand the problems of modern America, and what he could do to help solve them.

RUNNING FOR OFFICE: In 1996, Obama decided to run for the Illinois State Senate. He won, and served for eight years. While in the Illinois congress, he worked on

Obama introduces Joe Biden as his running mate, in Springfield, Illinois, August 23, 2008.

many issues. He championed tax cuts for working families and early childhood education.

In 2004, Obama decided to run for national office. He ran for the job of U.S. Senator from Illinois. He won, and became only the third African-American to hold the office of Senator.

That same year, he gave a speech at the Democratic National Convention. It was a moving and inspiring speech. He talked about America's problems. He also talked about how government can, and should help. Most of all, he talked about his hope for America, "the audacity of hope." Viewers were impressed with the young man from Illinois. They knew he had a bright future.

As a Senator, Obama serves on several special committees. These include Health, Education, Labor and Pensions; Foreign Relations; Veterans' Affairs; and Environment and Public Works.

RUNNING FOR THE DEMOCRATIC NOMINATION: In 2007, Obama decided to run for President. Virtually unknown to most Americans, he first needed to win the nomination of the Democratic Party. His main opponent was Hillary Clinton, wife of former President Bill Clinton and senator from New York.

Primaries: In American politics, Presidential candidates are selected for the Democratic and Republican tickets through "primaries." In primaries, voters cast ballots for delegates who are pledged to vote for one candidate. The delegates vote at the Party's convention, held the summer before the election.

Obama and Clinton were soon the frontrunners in the race. It was an historical contest. It was the first time that a woman and an African-American were fighting for the nomination of a major party. The two traveled and debated all over the country. Voters in primary states went to the polls to cast ballots. Many states had the

Obama with his family.

highest voter turnout in their history. Many Americans became engaged in the election. Young voters especially were drawn to Obama's message of hope and change.

RUNNING FOR PRESIDENT: By June 2008, Obama had won enough delegates to be declared the Presidential nominee of the Democratic Party. It was another historical moment. No black candidate had ever won the nomination of a major party before.

Obama's opponent in the race for President is John McCain (you can read a profile of McCain in this issue of *Biography for Beginners*). From now until the election in November, the two candidates will travel all over the country talking to Americans. They will also have debates that voters will watch on television.

Obama has some strong opinions about the current state of the country. He wants to bring about change in politics. He wants to get people from all political backgrounds involved, talking about the nation's problems. He wants to overcome the bitterness and anger that has been part of political races in the past.

Obama opposes the war in Iraq that began in 2003. He wants to end the conflict there and bring the troops home. He recently went on a tour of the Middle East and Europe. He visited troops and military leaders in Iraq and Afghanistan. In Europe, he gave speeches that outlined his vision for American foreign policy. He also is concerned about the economy, health care, education, and the environment.

CHOOSING A VICE PRESIDENT: In August, Obama chose Senator Joseph Biden to be his running mate as Vice President. Together, they are traveling the country speaking to voters.

BARACK OBAMA'S HOME AND FAMILY: Obama met his future wife, Michelle, in Chicago, when they worked for the same law firm. They have two daughters, Malia, who is 10, and Sasha, who is 7. The Obamas try to shield their daughters' privacy. Despite living in the "fishbowl" of a Presidential election, they try to find time just to be together and be themselves.

Obama still loves to play basketball. On the campaign trail, he tries to get in a game, sometimes with his staff or secret service agents.

BARACK OBAMA'S BOOKS:

Dreams from My Father
The Audacity of Hope

FOR MORE INFORMATION:

Write: Senator Barack Obama
    713 Hart Senate Office Building
    Washington, DC 20510

WORLD WIDE WEB SITES:

http://obama.senate.gov
http://www.barackobama.com/

QUOTE

"I'm asking you to believe. Not just in my ability to bring about real change in Washington. I'm asking you to believe in yours."

UPDATE

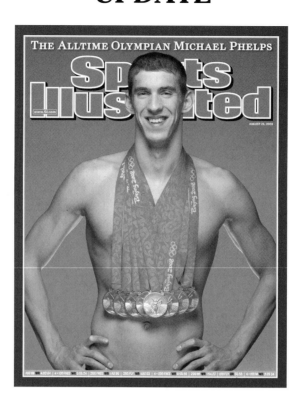

THE ALLTIME OLYMPIAN MICHAEL PHELPS

Michael Phelps
1985-
American Swimmer and Winner of Eight Gold Medals in the 2008 Olympics

[**Editor's Note:** Michael Phelps first appeared in *Biography for Beginners* in Spring 2006. This year, he made swimming history: he won eight gold medals, more than anyone in history, at the 2008 Olympics in Beijing. This update focuses on that historic achievement. For information on Phelps's early life, please read the entry in the Spring 2006 issue.]

THE 2008 OLYMPICS: Michael Phelps went into the 2008 Olympics with a lot of expectations. Sports fans everywhere wondered if he could do what had never been done before—win eight gold medals. The previous record of seven gold medals in one Olympics was held by another swimmer, Mark Spitz.

There was a huge amount of pressure on Phelps, especially from the media. With the whole world watching, Phelps went to Beijing, the site of the 2008 Olympics, and prepared for his events.

THE EVENTS: Every event Phelps swam was special, and every one had it's incredible moments.

FIRST GOLD: Phelps's first event was the 400-meter IM, or individual medley. That's one of the toughest races in swimming: 100 meters each of butterfly, backstroke, breaststroke, and freestyle. Not only did he come in first, he broke the world record. It was one of seven records he would break in the Olympics.

SECOND GOLD: Phelps's second gold came as part of a team in the men's 4 x 100 freestyle relay. The American swimmers were behind the French team by a body length on the last 50 meters. Then American Jason Lezak swam the race of his life. With Phelps and his teammates screaming, Lezak touched out the French team for the gold, and a world record.

THIRD GOLD: Phelps's next race was the 200-meter freestyle. Once again, he broke the world record as he came in first. The third gold was his.

FOURTH GOLD: Phelps's won his next race despite facing every swimmer's greatest fear. As he dove into the pool for the 200-meter butterfly, his goggles were loose and filled with water. He couldn't even see where he was for his turns, so he counted strokes. And when the event was done, he'd won, broken the world record, and added a fourth gold medal.

FIFTH GOLD: The next event in Phelps's incredible achievement was the 4 x 200 freestyle relay. Once again, the Americans beat the competition, capturing the gold and breaking the world record.

SIXTH GOLD: Phelps's sixth gold medal came in the 200-meter individual medley. The race included another world record for the swimmer some were calling the "Baltimore bullet."

SEVENTH GOLD: Phelps's seventh race was one of the most incredible of the Olympics. In the 100-meter butterfly, he was seventh at the turn. With 50 meters to go, Phelps put on a charge. When the race was over, Serb swimmer Milorad Cavic thought he had won the race, with Phelps second. But the camera told another story. Michael Phelps had touched out Cavic and won by an incredible 1/100th of a second. Fans around the world watched those last seconds in slow motion, over and over again, marveling at his achievement.

EIGHTH GOLD: Phelps's last race was again part of a relay, this time the 4 x 100 medley. The Americans dominated the race, and the team won. Phelps stood on the pool deck, with his arms wrapped around his teammates. He was overcome with emotion. He'd done what no one had ever done before—won an incredible eight gold medals in one Olympics.

Phelps was as gracious and humble as he could be. He thanked his teammates, his coach, and his family for all their support. His achievement was cheered by people all over the world. He'd wanted to bring worldwide attention to the sport of swimming, and he had surely done that, and more.

FUTURE PLANS: Phelps is taking some time off now. "I'm going to sit on the beach and do nothing," he says. He wants to try new things, too. "I'm going to try snowboarding. I want to try golf. I'm just going to experiment."

Phelps plans to get back in the pool in a few months, and will start competing again. As one of the greatest athletes of the era, he's got many endorsement contracts, too. He's moving back to Baltimore from Ann Arbor, Michigan, and continues to be coached by Bob Bowman.

FOR MORE INFORMATION ON MICHAEL PHELPS:

Write: USA Swimming
        1 Olympic Plaza
        Colorado Springs, CO 80909

WORLD WIDE WEB SITES:

http://www.michaelphelps.com
http://www.usaswimming.org

QUOTE

"If you dream as big as you can dream, anything is possible."

Name Index

Listed below are the names of all individuals who have appeared in *Biography for Beginners*, followed by the issue and year in which they appear.

Subject Index

This index includes subjects, occupations, and ethnic and minority origins for individuals who have appeared in *Biography for Beginners*.

O'Neal, Shaquille, Fall '95

Patrick, Danica, Fall 2005

Pele, Spring '97

Phelps, Michael, Spring 2006, Fall 2008

Ripken, Cal Jr., Fall, '96

Robinson, David, Fall '96

Scurry, Briana, Fall '99

Smith, Emmitt, Spring '95

Sosa, Sammy, Spring '99

Strug, Kerri, Spring '97

Suzuki, Ichiro, Fall 2003

Swoopes, Sheryl, Spring 2000

Van Dyken, Amy, Spring 2000

Vick, Michael, Spring 2003

Wie, Michelle, Spring 2004

Williams, Serena, Fall 2003

Woods, Tiger, Fall '98

Yamaguchi, Kristi, Fall '97

Austrian

Bemelmans, Ludwig, Spring 2004

Australian

Fox, Mem, Fall 2004

Irwin, Steve, Spring 2003

authors

Aliki, Spring '96

Angelou, Maya, Fall 2006

Applegate, K.A., Spring 2000

Avi, Spring 2003

Babbitt, Natalie, Spring 2006

Bemelmans, Ludwig, Spring 2004

Berenstain, Jan, Fall '95

Berenstain, Stan, Fall, '95

Blume, Judy, Fall '95

Brett, Jan, Spring '95

Bridwell, Norman, Fall '99

Brown, Marc, Spring '98

Brown, Margaret Wise, Spring 2006

Brunhoff, Jean de, Spring 2007

Bunting, Eve, Fall 2001

Burton, Virginia Lee, Spring '97

Byars, Betsy, Fall 2002

Cannon, Janell, Spring '99

Carle, Eric, Spring '95

Carson, Ben, Fall 2003

Christopher, Matt, Fall '97

Cleary, Beverly, Spring '95

Clements, Andrew, Spring 2005

Cole, Joanna, Fall '95

Collier, Bryan, Spring 2006

Cooney, Barbara, Spring 2001

Pinkney, Brian, Fall 2005

Pinkwater, Daniel, Spring 2000

Polacco, Patricia, Fall '97

Potter, Beatrix, Fall '98

Prelutsky, Jack, Spring '95

Raschka, Chris, Spring 2006

Rey, H. A., Fall 2006

Rey, Margret, Fall 2006

Ringgold, Faith, Spring '99

Rohmann, Eric, Spring 2004

Rowling, J.K., Fall 2000, Fall 2007

Rylant, Cynthia, Fall '96

Sabuda, Robert, Spring 2005

Sachar, Louis, Spring 2002

Scarry, Richard, Spring '95

Scieszka, Jon, Fall '95

Sendak, Maurice, Spring '96

Seuss, Dr., Spring '95

Shannon, David, Fall 2006

Silverstein, Shel, Spring '97

Sis, Peter, Fall 2004

Small, David, Fall 2002

Steig, William, Spring 2000

Van Allsburg, Chris, Spring '96

Viorst, Judith, Fall 2006

Wells, Rosemary, Spring '96

White, E.B., Spring 2002

Wiesner, David, Spring 2007

Wilder, Laura Ingalls, Fall '96

Willard, Nancy, Spring 2004

Williams, Garth, Fall '96

Willems, Mo, Spring 2007

Wood, Audrey, Spring 2003

Wood, Don, Spring 2003

Yolen, Jane, Spring '99

autobiographer

Angelou, Maya, Fall 2006

baseball players

Bonds, Barry, Fall 2002

Griffey, Ken Jr., Fall '95

Jeter, Derek, Fall 2000

Martinez, Pedro, Spring 2001

McGwire, Mark, Spring '99

Ripken, Cal Jr., Fall '96

Sosa, Sammy, Spring '99

Suzuki, Ichiro, Fall 2003

basketball players

Bryant, Kobe, Fall '99

Lucid, Shannon, Fall '97

MacLachlan, Patricia, Spring 2003

Martin, Ann M., Spring '96

McKissack, Patricia, Fall '98

Miller, Shannon, Spring '95

Moceanu, Dominique, Fall '98

Nechita, Alexandra, Spring 2000

Numeroff, Laura, Fall '99

Ochoa, Ellen, Spring 2005

O'Donnell, Rosie, Fall '99

Oleynik, Larisa, Spring '96

Olsen, Ashley, Spring '95

Olsen, Mary-Kate, Spring '95

Osborne, Mary Pope, Fall 2001

Parish, Peggy, Spring '97

Park, Barbara, Spring '98

Parks, Rosa, Fall '95

Paterson, Katherine, Spring 2007

Patrick, Danica, Fall 2005

Pinkney, Andrea Davis, Fall 2004

Polacco, Patricia, Fall '97

Potter, Beatrix, Fall '98

Raven, Spring 2004

Rey, Margret, Fall 2006

Rice, Condoleezza, Spring 2002

Ringgold, Faith, Spring '99

Rowling, J.K., Fall 2000; Revised, Fall 2007

Rylant, Cynthia, Fall '96

Scurry, Briana, Fall '99

Strug, Kerri, Spring '97

Swoopes, Sheryl, Spring 2000

Teresa, Mother, Fall '98

Van Dyken, Amy, Spring 2000

Viorst, Judith, Fall 2006

Watson, Emma, Fall 2004

Wells, Rosemary, Spring '96

Wie, Michelle, Spring 2004

Wilder, Laura Ingalls, Fall '96

Willard, Nancy, Spring 2004

Williams, Serena, Fall 2003

Wilson, Mara, Spring '97

Winfrey, Oprah, Fall 2002

Wood, Audrey, Spring 2003

Yamaguchi, Kristi, Fall '97

Yolen, Jane, Spring '99

film director

Parks, Gordon, Spring 2007

Swedish

Lindgren, Astrid, Fall 2002

swimmers

Coughlin, Natalie, Fall 2008

Phelps, Michael, Spring 2006, Fall 2008

Van Dyken, Amy, Spring 2000

television

Allen, Tim, Fall '96

Brandy, Fall '96

Bryan, Zachery Ty, Spring '97

Burton, LeVar, Spring '98

Bynes, Amanda, Spring 2005

Cannon, Nick, Spring 2003

Couric, Katie, Spring 2007

Cyrus, Miley, Fall 2007

Duff, Hilary, Spring 2003

Efron, Zac, Fall 2006

Ellerbee, Linda, Fall 2003

Hart, Melissa Joan, Fall '95

Hudgens, Vanessa Anne, Spring 2007

Irwin, Steve, Spring 2003

Lewis, Shari, Spring '99

Muniz, Frankie, Fall 2001

Nye, Bill, Spring '99

O'Donnell, Rosie, Fall '99

Oleynik, Larisa, Spring '96

Olsen, Ashley, Spring '95

Olsen, Mary-Kate, Spring '95

Raven, Spring 2004

Rogers, Fred, Fall '98

Thomas, Jonathan Taylor, Fall '95

White, Jaleel, Fall '97

Winfrey, Oprah, Fall 2002

tennis

Williams, Serena, Fall 2003

United Nations

Annan, Kofi, Fall 2000

Vice President of the United States

Cheney, Dick, Fall 2003

Gore, Al, Fall '97

Birthday Index

January

7 Katie Couric (1957)
8 Stephen Hawking (1942)
12 John Lasseter (1957)
14 Shannon Lucid (1943)
17 Shari Lewis (1934)
21 Hakeem Olajuwon (1963)
26 Vince Carter (1977)
28 Wayne Gretzky (1961)
29 Bill Peet (1915)
   Rosemary Wells (1943)
   Oprah Winfrey (1954)
30 Dick Cheney (1941)
31 Bryan Collier (1967)

February

1 Hughes: Feb. 1 (1902)
2 Judith Viorst (1931)
4 Rosa Parks (1913)
5 David Wiesner (1956)
7 Laura Ingalls Wilder (1867)
9 Wilson "Snowflake" Bentley (1865)
11 Jane Yolen (1939)
   Brandy (1979)
12 Judy Blume (1938)
   David Small (1945)
13 Mary GrandPré (1954)
15 Norman Bridwell (1928)
   Amy Van Dyken (1973)
16 LeVar Burton (1957)
17 Michael Jordan (1963)
22 Steve Irwin (1962)
24 Steven Jobs (1955)
27 Chelsea Clinton (1980)

March

2 Leo Dillon (1933)
   Dr. Seuss (1904)
   David Satcher (1941)
3 Patricia MacLachlan (1938)
   Jackie Joyner-Kersee (1962)
4 Garrett Morgan (1877)
   Dav Pilkey (1966)
5 Mem Fox (1946)
   Jake Lloyd (1989)
6 Chris Raschka (1959)

23 Margaret Wise Brown (1910)

29 Andrew Clements (1949)

June

2 Freddy Adu (1989)

5 Richard Scarry (1919)

6 Cynthia Rylant (1954)
Larisa Oleynik (1981)
Tim Berners-Lee (1955)

9 Freddie Highmore (1992)

10 Maurice Sendak (1928)
Tara Lipinski (1982)

11 Joe Montana (1956)

13 Tim Allen (1953)

15 Jack Horner (1946)

18 Chris Van Allsburg (1949)

25 Eric Carle (1929)

26 Nancy Willard (1936)
Derek Jeter (1974)
Michael Vick (1980)

30 Robert Ballard (1971)
Michael Phelps (1985)

July

2 Dave Thomas (1932)

6 George W. Bush (1946)

7 Lisa Leslie (1972)
Michelle Kwan (1980)

11 E.B. White (1899)
Patricia Polacco (1944)

12 Kristi Yamaguchi (1972)

13 Stephanie Kwolek (1923)

14 Peggy Parish (1927)

14 Laura Numeroff (1953)

18 Nelson Mandela (1918)

24 Barry Bonds (1964)
Mara Wilson (1987)

26 Jan Berenstain (1923)

28 Beatrix Potter (1866)
Natalie Babbitt (1932)
Jim Davis (1945)

31 J.K. Rowling (1965)
Daniel Radcliffe (1989)

August

2 Betsy Byars (1928)

3 Tom Brady (1977)

4 Jeff Gordon (1971)
Obama: Aug 4 (1961)

6 Barbara Cooney (1917)
David Robinson (1965)

9 Patricia McKissack (1944)
Whitney Houston (1963)

11 Joanna Cole (1944)

12 Walter Dean Myers (1937)

Fredrick McKissack (1939)

Ann M. Martin (1955)

15 Linda Ellerbee (1944)

16 Matt Christopher (1917)

18 Paula Danziger (1944)

19 Bill Clinton (1946)

21 Stephen Hillenburg (1961)

23 Kobe Bryant (1978)

Coughlin: Aug. 23 (1982)

24 Cal Ripken Jr. (1960)

26 Mother Teresa (1910)

27 Alexandra Nechita (1985)

28 Brian Pinkney (1961)

29 Temple Grandin (1947)

McCain: Aug. 29 (1936)

30 Virginia Lee Burton (1909)

Sylvia Earle (1935)

Donald Crews (1938)

31 Itzhak Perlman (1945)

September

1 Gloria Estefan (1958)

3 Aliki (1929)

7 Briana Scurry (1971)

8 Jack Prelutsky (1940)

Jon Scieszka (1954)

Jonathan Taylor Thomas (1982)

15 McCloskey, Robert (1914)

Tomie dePaola (1934)

16 H. A. Rey (1898)

Roald Dahl (1916)

17 Kevin Clash (1960)

18 Ben Carson (1951)

Lance Armstrong (1971)

24 Jim Henson (1936)

25 Andrea Davis Pinkney (1963)

25 Will Smith (1968)

26 Serena Williams (1981)

28 Hilary Duff (1987)

29 Stan Berenstain (1923)

30 Dominique Moceanu (1981)

October

1 Mark McGwire (1963)

5 Grant Hill (1972)

Maya Lin (1959)

6 Lonnie Johnson (1949)

7 Yo-Yo Ma (1955)

8 Faith Ringgold (1930)

9 Zachery Ty Bryan (1981)

10 James Marshall (1942)

11 Michelle Wie (1989)

12 Marion Jones (1975)
13 Nancy Kerrigan (1969)
17 Mae Jemison (1954)
Nick Cannon (1980)
18 Wynton Marsalis (1961)
Zac Efron (1987)
22 Ichiro Suzuki (1973)
23 Pele (1940)
25 Pedro Martinez (1971)
26 Hillary Clinton (1947)
26 Steven Kellogg (1941)
Eric Rohmann (1957)
28 Bill Gates (1955)
31 Katherine Paterson (1932)

November

3 Janell Cannon (1957)
4 Laura Bush (1946)
9 Lois Ehlert (1934)
12 Sammy Sosa (1968)
14 Astrid Lindgren (1907)
William Steig (1907)
Condoleezza Rice (1954)
15 Daniel Pinkwater (1941)
19 Savion Glover (1973)

Kerri Strug (1977)
Ken Griffey Jr. (1969)
23 Miley Cyrus (1992)
25 Marc Brown (1946)
26 Charles Schulz (1922)
27 Bill Nye (1955)
Kevin Henkes (1960)
Jaleel White (1977)
30 Gordon Parks (1912)

December

1 Jan Brett (1949)
5 Frankie Muniz (1985)
9 Jean de Brunhoff (1899)
10 Raven (1985)
18 Christina Aguilera (1980)
14 Vanessa Anne Hudgens (1988)
19 Eve Bunting (1928)
22 Jerry Pinkney (1939)
23 Avi (1937)
26 Susan Butcher (1954)
30 LeBron James (1984)
Mercer Mayer (1943)
Tiger Woods (1975)

Photo and Illustration Credits

Natalie Coughlin/Photos: Courtesy USA Swimming; AP Images.

Ella Fitzgerald/Photos: Courtesy of the Library of Congress; AP Images.

Jennifer L. Holm and Matthew Holm/Photo: Jodie Otte, courtesy Random House; Covers: OUR ONLY MAY AMELIA copyright © 1999 by Jennifer L. Holm; PENNY FROM HEAVEN copyright © 2006 by Jennifer L. Holm; BABYMOUSE: QUEEN OF THE WORLD copyright © 2005 by Jennifer and Matthew Holm; BABYMOUSE: MONSTER MASH copyright © 2007 by Jennifer and Matthew Holm; BABYMOUSE: THE MUSICAL copyright © 2008 by Jennifer and Matthew Holm.

Langston Hughes: Courtesy of the Library of Congress; THE DREAM KEEPER AND OTHER POEMS text copyright © 1932 by Alfred A. Knopf; renewed 1960 by Langston Hughes; illustrations copyright 1994 by Brian Pinkney. POETRY FOR YOUNG PEOPLE copyright © 1994 by the Estate of Langston Hughes. Artwork c 2006 by Benny Andrews.

John McCain/Photos: Office of U.S. Senator John McCain; Newscom.com; AP Images.

Barack Obama/Photos: Office of U.S. Senator Barack Obama; AP Images.

Michael Phelps/Photos: Getty Images.